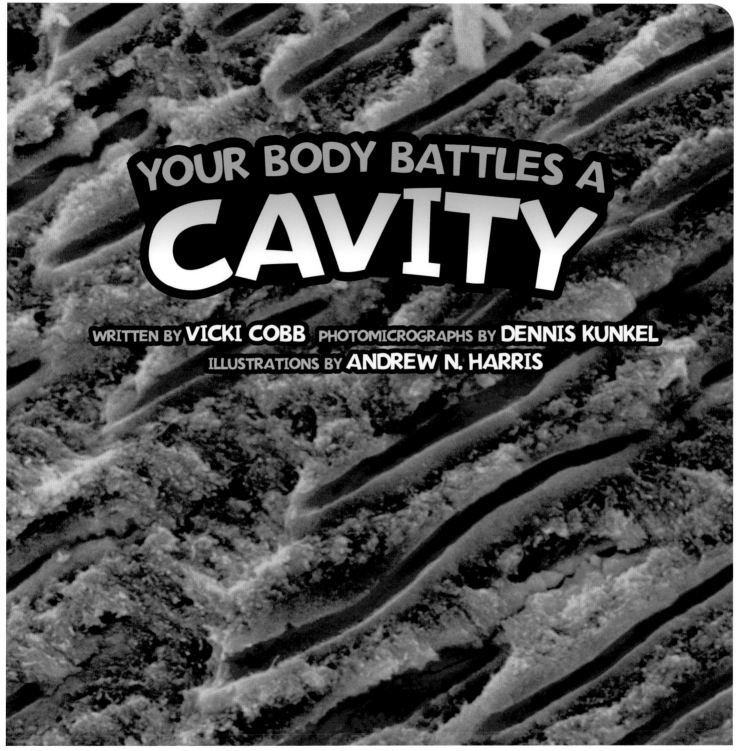

YOUR BODY BATTLES A
CAVITY

WRITTEN BY **VICKI COBB**   PHOTOMICROGRAPHS BY **DENNIS KUNKEL**
ILLUSTRATIONS BY **ANDREW N. HARRIS**

M Millbrook Press / Minneapolis

NOTE: The photomicrographs in this book were taken with a scanning electron microscope (SEM). The photos are originally in black and white. A computer program is used to add color, often to highlight interesting features. The colors used do not show the real colors of the subject. The $\times$ followed by a number indicates magnification. For example, $\times250$ means the object in the picture is 250 times larger than its real size.

The author thanks Lori A. Auster, D.D.S., White Plains, NY; Jan Hu, B.D.S., Ph.D., University of Michigan, School of Dentistry; and Dr. David Koss, pediatric dentist, for their invaluable technical advice. The author also thanks Mary Slamin and Gail Fell, children's librarians from the Greenburgh, New York, Public Library for assistance with the Further Reading list.

For Jillian Davis Cobb —VC

This series is dedicated to my mom, Carmen Kunkel, for the care she gives her children and grandchildren —DK

For my father, Jay, and brother Mark, the best dentists in the world—ANH

Millbrook Press
A division of Lerner Publishing Group, Inc.
241 First Avenue North
Minneapolis, MN 55401 U.S.A.

Website address: www.lernerbooks.com

Library of Congress Cataloging-in-Publication Data

Cobb, Vicki.
    Your body battles a cavity / by Vicki Cobb ; with photomicrographs by Dennis Kunkel ; illustrations by Andrew N. Harris.
        p. cm. — (Body Battles)
    Includes bibliographical references and index.
    ISBN 978-0-8225-7469-9 (lib. bdg. : alk. paper)
    1. Teeth—Care and hygiene—Juvenile literature. 2. Dental caries—Juvenile literature. I. Harris, Andrew, 1977– ill. II. Title.
RK63.C63 2009
617.6'01—dc22   2008002827

Manufactured in the United States of America
1 2 3 4 5 6 – DP – 14 13 12 11 10 09

You never want to have a toothache! It hurts so much that you can't think about anything else. A toothache means that trouble has been brewing in your mouth for a long time. Months, even years, earlier a toothache starts out as a small damaged spot called a cavity. Cavities, also called tooth decay, don't have to happen—which means that toothaches don't have to happen. Meet the superheroes of your body that work with you to help keep your teeth healthy. This book tells their story.

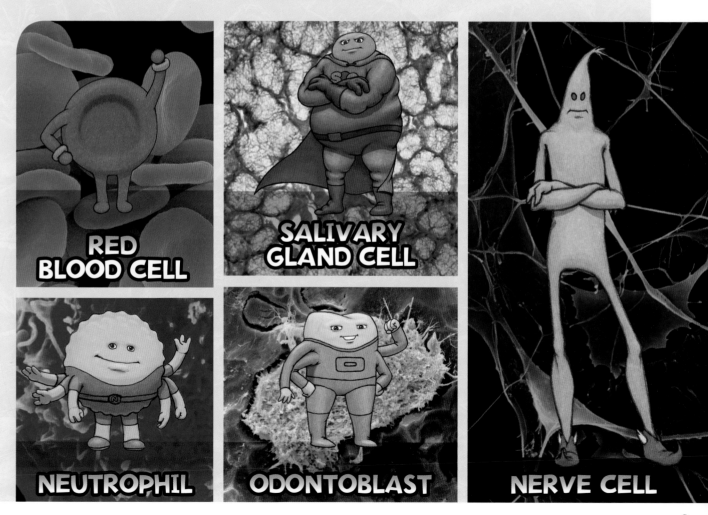

RED
BLOOD CELL

SALIVARY
GLAND CELL

NEUTROPHIL

ODONTOBLAST

NERVE CELL

Your whole body, even parts of your teeth, is made of tiny living things called cells. Cells are so tiny that they can only be seen with a microscope—a very powerful magnifying glass. Different cells do different jobs.

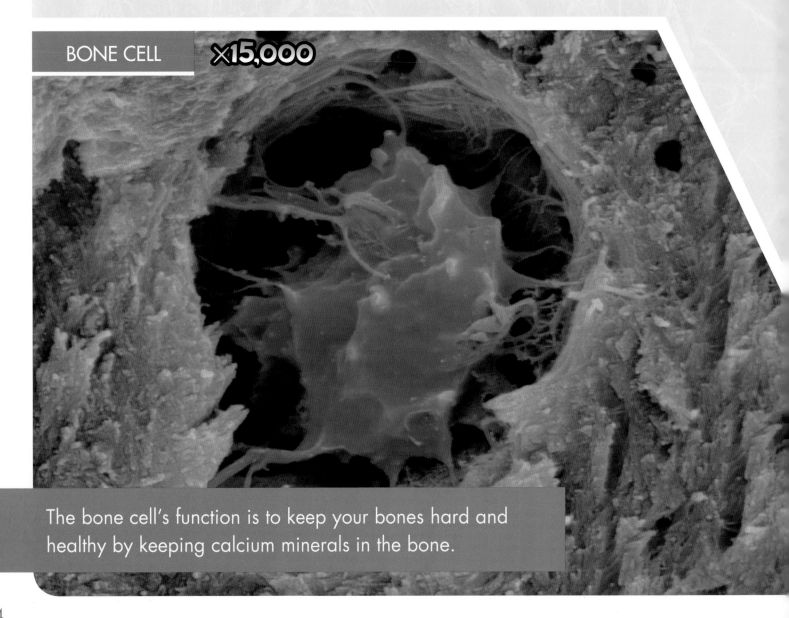

BONE CELL ✕15,000

The bone cell's function is to keep your bones hard and healthy by keeping calcium minerals in the bone.

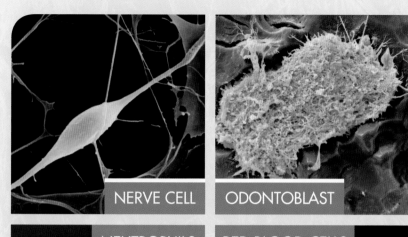

NERVE CELL ODONTOBLAST

NEUTROPHILS RED BLOOD CELLS

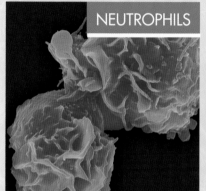
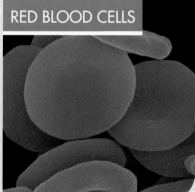

When you get a toothache, germs are attacking certain cells deep inside your tooth. This is how it all happens.

A cavity begins on the enamel, a tooth's outermost layer. Enamel is the hardest substance of the human body—even harder than bone.

Just under the enamel is another hard material called dentin.

The center of the tooth is a soft area containing blood and nerves. This is called the pulp.

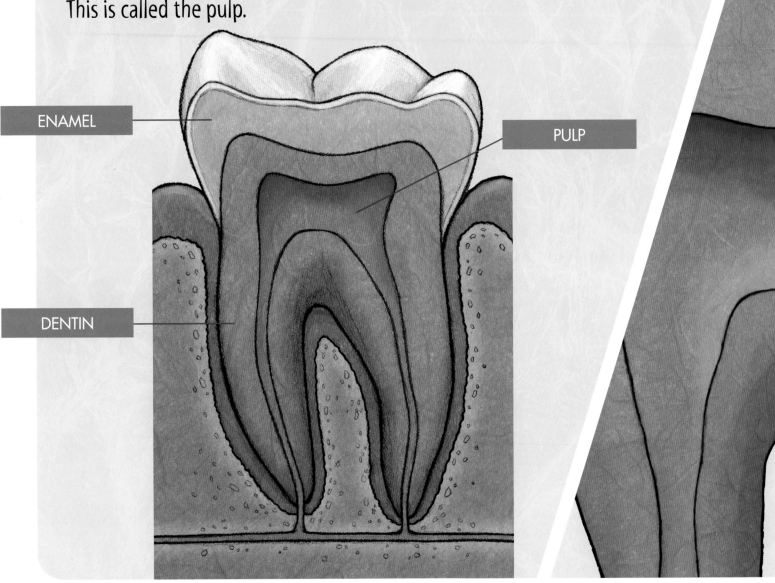

ENAMEL

PULP

DENTIN

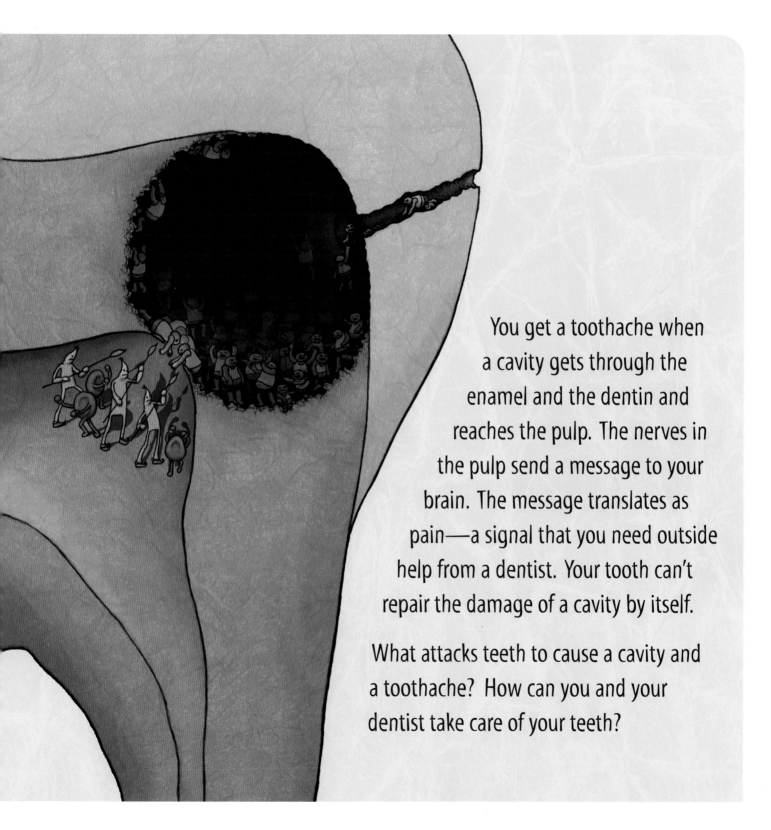

You get a toothache when a cavity gets through the enamel and the dentin and reaches the pulp. The nerves in the pulp send a message to your brain. The message translates as pain—a signal that you need outside help from a dentist. Your tooth can't repair the damage of a cavity by itself.

What attacks teeth to cause a cavity and a toothache? How can you and your dentist take care of your teeth?

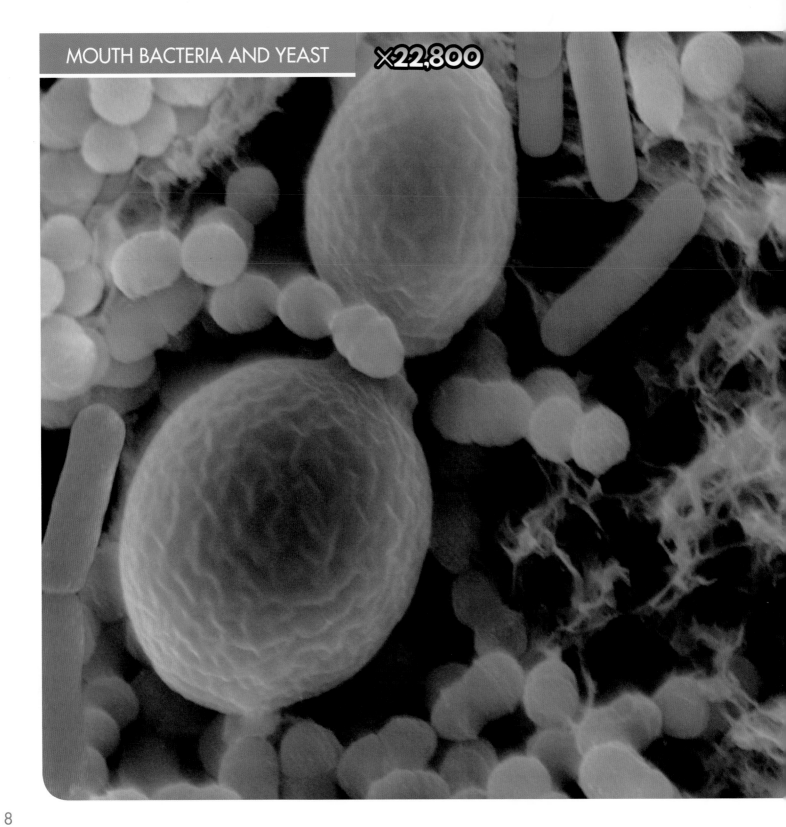

Bacteria are one-celled living things. They enter your mouth on the food you eat and in the air you breathe. Many kinds of bacteria wind up in your mouth, but the ones that cause cavities are round bacteria called *Streptococcus mutans*. They thrive in your warm, moist mouth. They produce a kind of glue so that they stick to the surface of your teeth and to one another. The combination of the sticky bacteria and their acid waste products as well as saliva make up a coating called plaque.

These are some of the germs that live in your mouth. The round cells are the strep bacteria. The long pink cells are another type of bacteria and the big yellowish bodies are yeasts.

So what does plaque do? Talk about a monster in the mouth! Plaque on your teeth, especially around your gums, lets the bacteria settle there, giving them plenty of time to cause cavities. When you wake up in the morning, it's the overnight accumulation of plaque that make your teeth feel a little furry.

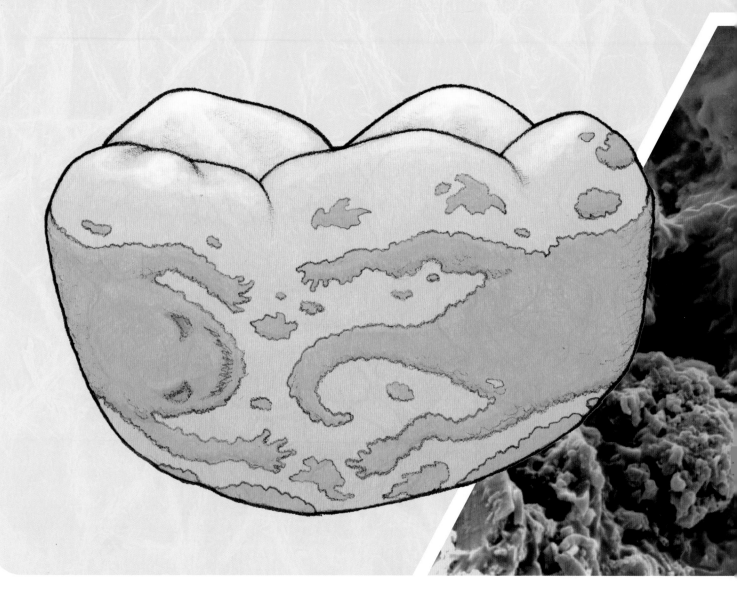

If you want to actually see where your own plaque is on your teeth, you can buy a mouthwash for kids at your pharmacy. It stains the plaque so you can see exactly where to scrub it away. If that plaque isn't removed by brushing and flossing, it can change into tartar and lead to cavities.

X4,410

PLAQUE AND TARTAR

Plaque, shown in the bright red area along the top of the photo-micrograph, is soft and sticky. If it isn't removed, calcium minerals make it hard. Calcified plaque is called tartar. In this picture, the dark pink material is newly developed tartar, the brown areas are mineralized tartar, and the dark red area at the right is older tartar.

In the plaque, the strep bacteria are busy eating sugar that's in your mouth and making acid as a waste product. Acid is bad news for your teeth! It can stay on the surface of a tooth for a long time. The acid will eat away at your tooth, causing a microscopic rough spot on the enamel.

As the rough spot gets deeper, it becomes a tiny cave for more bacteria. They live and multiply in the cavity, doubling in number every twenty minutes! The more bacteria there are, the more acid they produce to eat away at the enamel until the hole reaches the dentin. Eventually the acid eats all the way through the dentin as well, causing a full-blown toothache when it reaches the pulp.

The good news is that you do have a first line of defense against cavities—saliva. Saliva is secreted by cells in salivary glands in your mouth. It is mostly water, but it also contains some proteins that harm acids. You make between 0.8 to 1.6 quarts (0.8 to 1.5 liters) of saliva a day! It constantly washes your teeth.

Saliva also contains a kind of protein, called an enzyme, that changes starch to sugar. Starch (which is found in foods such as potatoes and bread) is made up of long chains of sugar molecules. The enzyme in saliva starts breaking up these chains so that sugar can be absorbed into the blood. It's the first step in digestion—but the bad news is that it can also be the first step of a cavity. Some of this sugar stays in your mouth and can become food for the strep.

Here's an experiment you can do with one of your baby teeth. Put it in a small amount of cola for three or four days. Then look at your tooth. The enamel is eaten away by the acid in the soda, and the underlying dentin is completely exposed. Also, you can put a baby tooth into two tablespoons of white vinegar (another type of acid) and leave the container uncovered. If you wait long enough, the vinegar will completely evaporate. You will see a white powder on the bottom of the dish. This powder is the calcium mineral that makes the enamel so hard. The acid took the mineral out! This may take a week or two.

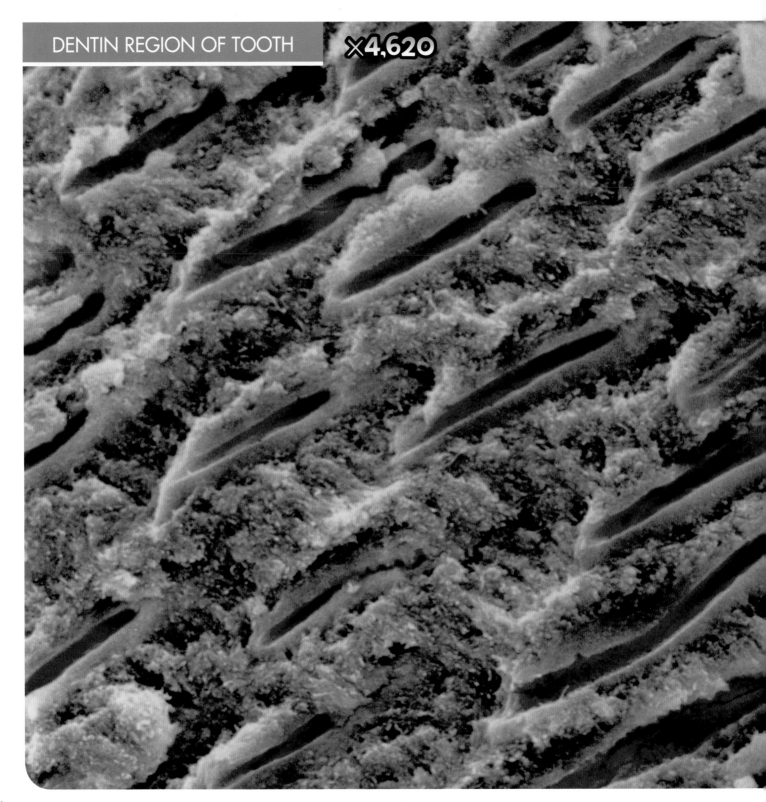

×4,620

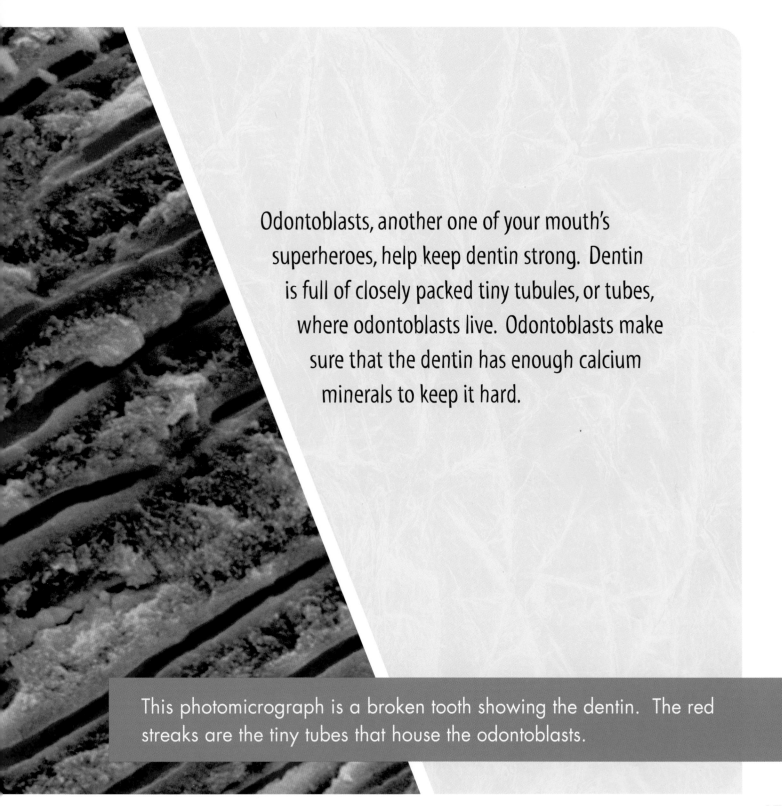

Odontoblasts, another one of your mouth's superheroes, help keep dentin strong. Dentin is full of closely packed tiny tubules, or tubes, where odontoblasts live. Odontoblasts make sure that the dentin has enough calcium minerals to keep it hard.

This photomicrograph is a broken tooth showing the dentin. The red streaks are the tiny tubes that house the odontoblasts.

Odontoblasts create dentin throughout your life to keep each tooth healthy. If a tooth gets a cavity, the odontoblast makes a special dentin to slow down the infection and protect the pulp. But in time, the special dentin can be overcome by the bacteria. If the tooth isn't fixed by a dentist, even the special dentin will be destroyed and ultimately the bacteria will win.

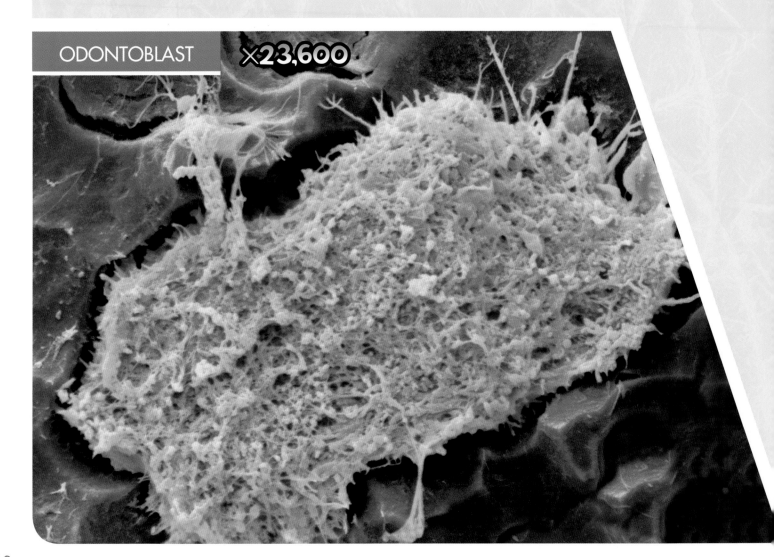

ODONTOBLAST ✕23,600

The center of your tooth is hollow and contains the pulp. The pulp is the main living part of the tooth. It is made up of nerves and blood vessels that extend into the tiny tubes in the dentin where the odontoblasts live. The blood brings food and oxygen to the odontoblasts. The nerves help you feel your teeth and sense the pain of a toothache.

Nerves are like one-way telephone wires to your brain. Nerves in your teeth sense pressure when you chew. They can also sense temperature. Breathe in with your mouth open, and sense the cool air on your teeth. When a cavity is deep enough to irritate the nerves, they send the message of pain to your brain.

When acid first eats through a tooth's enamel to the dentin, the tiny nerves in the dentin make the tooth sensitive to cold and to sweets. You don't yet have a toothache, but your tooth can experience flashes of pain.

After a while, however, the acid kills the nerves in the dentin. You don't feel any pain or sensitivity with a deep cavity until it reaches the pulp. Once that happens, bacteria attack the blood and nerve cells in the pulp. Blood rushes in to help fight the bacteria. The red blood cells bring oxygen, and the white blood cells called neutrophils fight the infection. The pressure from all the extra blood squeezes the nerves, and you have a toothache.

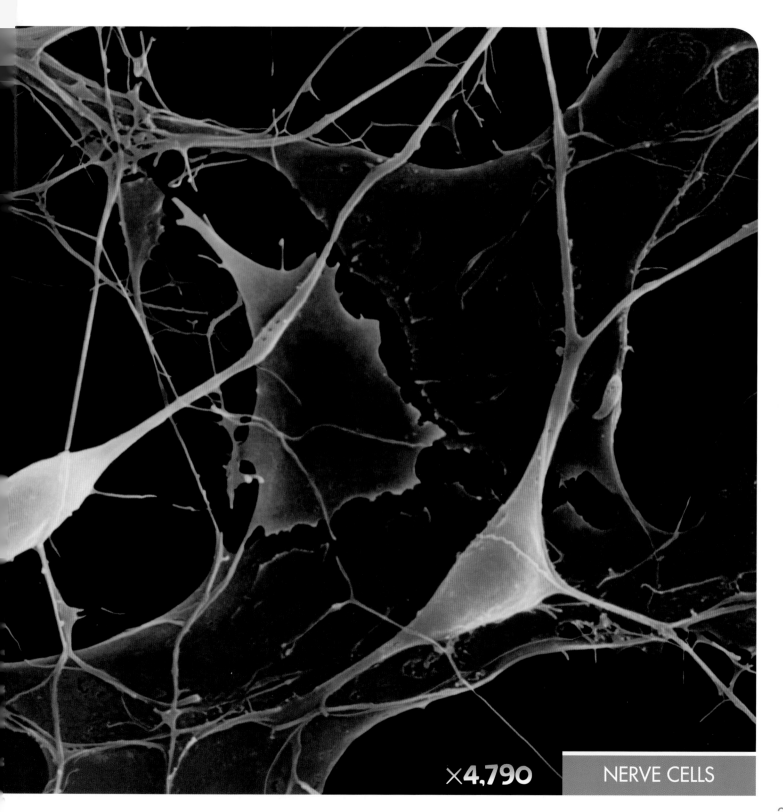

×**4,790**

NERVE CELLS

The best thing that you can do to prevent a cavity is to starve the bacteria by reducing the amount of sweets you eat. Brushing your teeth regularly to get rid of the plaque is a big help. Flossing is another good way to clean out the bacteria and plaque between your teeth. In addition, a mineral that can help prevent tooth decay is fluoride. Fluoride occurs naturally in the water you drink. If local water supply doesn't have enough, it can be added by the water company. While your teeth are being formed, fluoride from drinking water ends up in the enamel and makes it harder for acid to eat it away.

WARNING: FLUORIDE MAY BE SLIPPERY!

Scientists have also found that fluoride can prevent tooth decay if you use it in toothpaste or mouthwash. They are not sure how fluoride works—but they are quite sure that it does work.

Some dentists also put a seal on teeth to protect against bacteria. But this only protects the pits and grooves on tooth surfaces. It doesn't protect the flat sides, especially between teeth. That's why flossing is important.

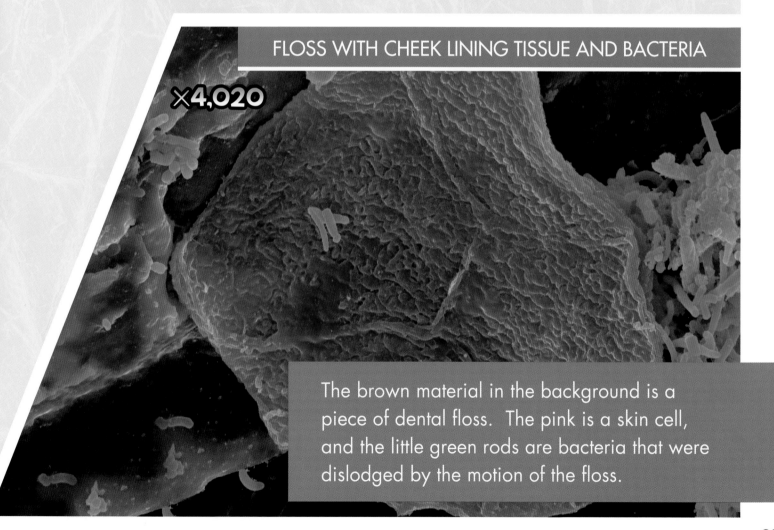

FLOSS WITH CHEEK LINING TISSUE AND BACTERIA

×4,020

The brown material in the background is a piece of dental floss. The pink is a skin cell, and the little green rods are bacteria that were dislodged by the motion of the floss.

Your tooth cannot repair a cavity on its own. A dentist must do the job. A dentist can treat a small cavity, so that it will never be able to spread deep enough into the tooth to reach the pulp, an event no one wants to experience!

A dentist examines your teeth with a sharp, pointed tool and a mirror, looking for cavities. If the enamel is thin when the tool presses, the dentist can tell if the soft spot is a cavity.

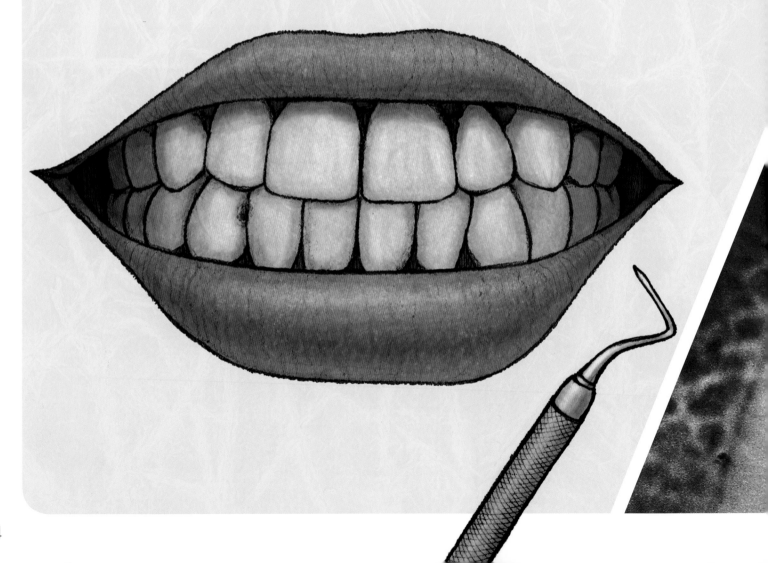

But some cavities are too small to see or feel. They may be hidden between the teeth or under the gum. So a dentist takes X-rays— pictures that can show cavities between teeth as well as the part hidden by the gum. Small cavities show up as a shadow on an X-ray.

The cavity on the tooth on the left has eaten through the enamel and much of the dentin, reaching the pulp. This patient is probably in pain!

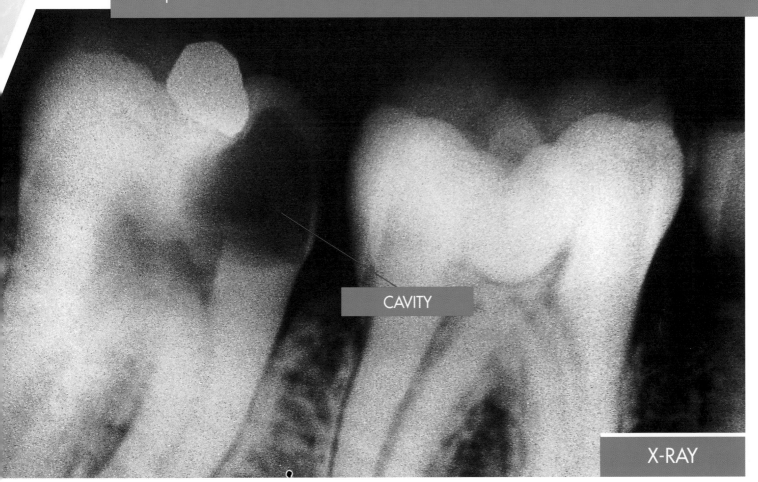

CAVITY

X-RAY

The dentist repairs your cavity by drilling a smooth clean hole where the cavity is. The drill removes the enamel and any part of the decay that has spread into the dentin. The spinning drill can heat up your tooth by friction, much as rubbing your hands together quickly warms them.

DRILL BIT WITH DIAMONDS ×35

Because tooth enamel is so hard, only something harder can cut it. The green stones are tiny pieces of diamond, the hardest material on earth. Nothing is too good for our teeth!

A spray shoots cool water over the drill and your tooth. A tube that's a vacuum for water removes the water from the bottom of your mouth while the dentist works. If the dentist is going to do a lot of drilling, you may get a shot of a drug that numbs your tooth. Dentists are trained to make sure that you don't feel pain while they work on your teeth!

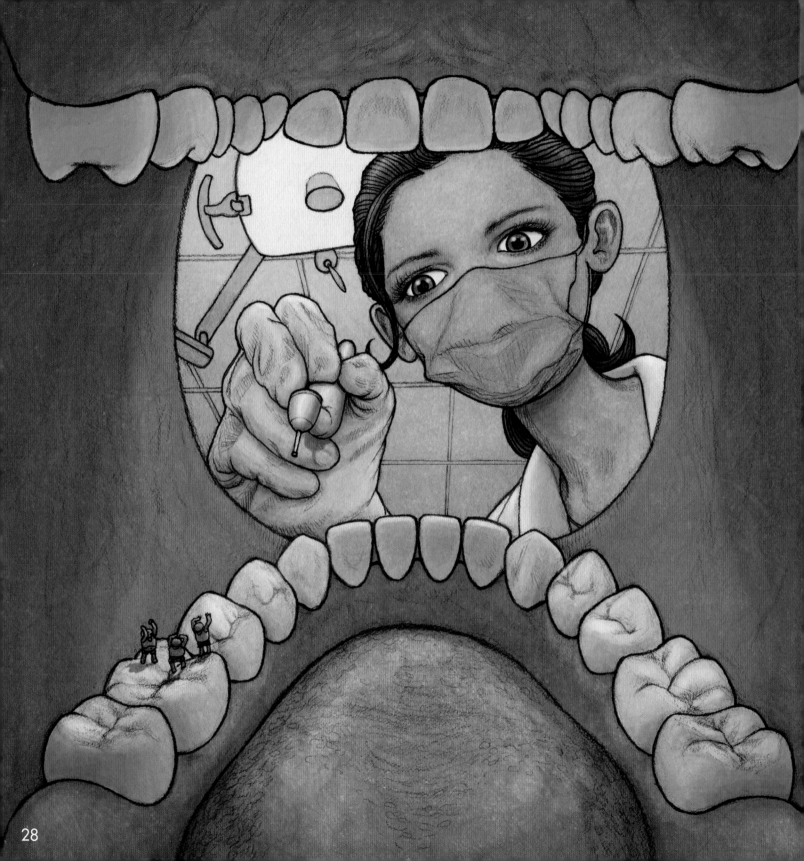

The drilled hole is cleaned out, removing any possible bacteria.
The hole is filled with a soft material that hardens once it's in place.
Some of these materials need a few minutes of light to make them hard.
You and your body can prevent cavities from starting, but if the germs
do get control, your dentist can repair the damage before you ever have
to suffer a toothache!

GLOSSARY

acid: a sour-tasting solution that can etch away tooth enamel over the years

bacteria: one-celled microorganisms that live with other living things. Some bacteria are helpful, but others cause disease.

calcium: a metallic element that combines with other elements to form minerals. Calcium minerals make tooth enamel hard. Milk and dairy products are a good source of calcium.

cavity: an area of tooth enamel that has been eaten away by acid

cells: the smallest units of all living things considered to be alive. The smallest living things have only one cell. Human beings are multicelled.

crown: the part of the tooth that sticks up above the gum line

dentin: the bonelike material that makes up most of a tooth under the enamel of the crown and surrounding the pulp. It absorbs the force of chewing.

dentist: a doctor who diagnoses tooth disease and repairs teeth

enamel: the white, translucent material covering the crowns of your teeth. It is the hardest, most mineralized substance in the human body.

fluoride: compounds containing the element fluorine, a nonmetal. Fluorides have been put into public drinking water to prevent cavities in children.

microscope: a powerful magnifier that allows us to look at cells. There are two main kinds of microscopes:

electron microscopes use electrons and can magnify even smaller structures. There are two types of electron microscopes—scanning (SEM), which can magnify up to 500,000 times, and transmission (TEM), which can magnify up to one million times.

optical microscopes use light and can magnify up to 1,500 times the actual size.

molecule: the smallest part of a substance that has all the properties of that substance. Molecules are made up of atoms.

odontoblasts: cells that form dentin and maintain the health of dentin throughout your life

plaque: a mixture of saliva, bacteria, and food that coats teeth. The bacteria in plaque give off acid that can cause cavities. Plaque can be removed by brushing and flossing teeth.

pulp: the soft center of a tooth. It is full of blood vessels and nerves. It also contains the odontoblasts that maintain the health of the tooth.

saliva: the watery substance produced in the mouth to protect the mouth, tongue, and teeth; to help you taste your food; and to start the digestion of food

X-ray: a photograph that shows the inside of your teeth. Dentists can see cavities at the earliest stage in an X-ray.

FURTHER READING

Ferguson, Beth. *Teeth.* New York: Benchmark Books, 2003.

Gower, Timothy. *This Book Bites!: Or Why Your Mouth Is More Than Just a Hole in Your Head.* Reading, MA: Planet Dexter, 1999.

Rice, Judith. *Those Icky Sticky Smelly Cavity-Causing But . . . Invisible Germs.* Topeka, KS: Tandem Library, 1997.

Silverstein, Alvin, Virginia B. Silverstein, and Laura Silverstein Nunn. *Tooth Decay and Cavities.* New York: Franklin Watts, 2000.

WEBSITES

Taking Care of Your Teeth
http://www.kidshealth.org/kid/stay_healthy/body/teeth.html
This site offers kid-friendly facts about dental hygiene.

Tooth Decay in Younger Kids Is Getting Worse
http://www.youtube.com/watch?v=CmaKKt0N8rQ
A news video shows how kids are getting cavities from sugared soft drinks.

The Truth about Teeth
http://www.kidshealth.com/kid/body/teeth_noSW.html
A description of tooth anatomy and types of teeth are included.

INDEX